How to get Seriously Rich while Failing in Business

How to get Seriously Rich while Failing in Business

The Fat Cat's guide to Management

Philip Sadler

Drawings by John Jensen

Souvenir Press

Contents

1. Getting started

Different people have different goals in life. Some want just to be happy, some to be famous, some want excitement and danger, some want to serve mankind and others want to become seriously rich. If you are in this last group this book is written for you.

Whatever your goal in life you are unlikely to achieve it by drifting along without a clear strategy. Realising one's ambitions takes planning, tactics and hard work – though the amount of actual hard work can be minimised. Start by sitting down and making a flow chart along the lines of the one on the next page, showing the actions you need to take and the stages through which you must pass en route to your goal. Your own chart will need to be more detailed and tailored to your own circumstances.

Charting your path to your goal – becoming seriously rich
The aspiring fat cat's flow chart

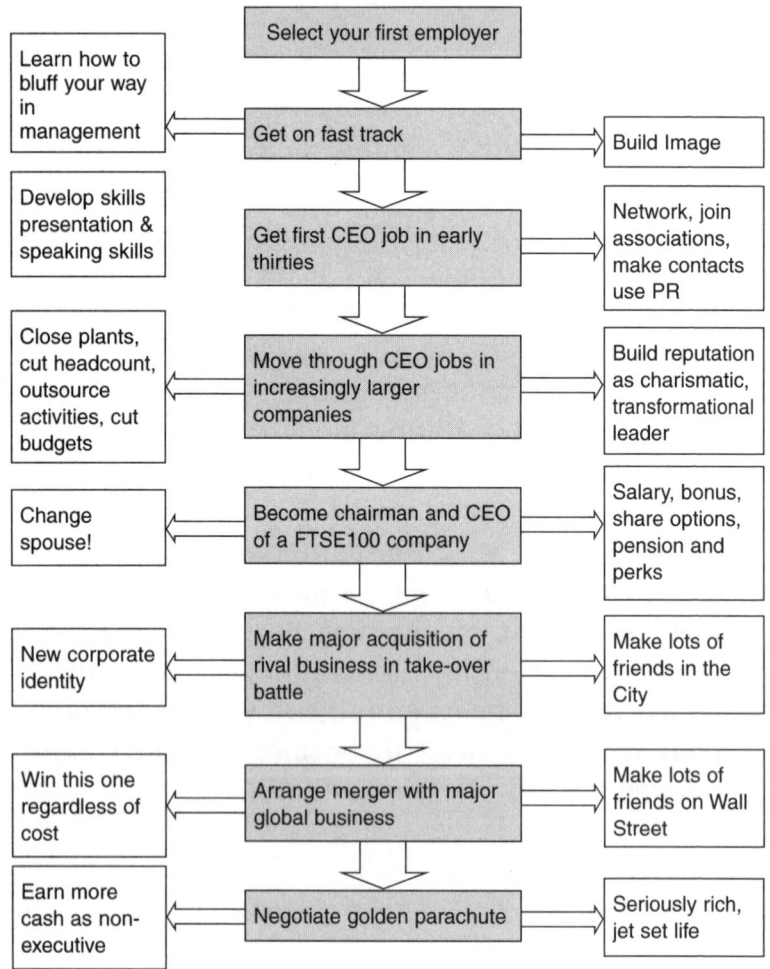

Learn how to bluff your way in management	Select your first employer	
	Get on fast track	Build Image
Develop skills presentation & speaking skills	Get first CEO job in early thirties	Network, join associations, make contacts use PR
Close plants, cut headcount, outsource activities, cut budgets	Move through CEO jobs in increasingly larger companies	Build reputation as charismatic, transformational leader
Change spouse!	Become chairman and CEO of a FTSE100 company	Salary, bonus, share options, pension and perks
New corporate identity	Make major acquisition of rival business in take-over battle	Make lots of friends in the City
Win this one regardless of cost	Arrange merger with major global business	Make lots of friends on Wall Street
Earn more cash as non-executive	Negotiate golden parachute	Seriously rich, jet set life

The first steps – becoming a top cat

To become a fat cat you first have to become a top cat.

There are two ways to do this – one easy and one hard.

The easy way

The easy way is simply to marry the daughter of the chairman or the owner of the business; this is a time-honoured fast track route to the top. Daughters usually get their own way with their indulgent fathers and this will almost certainly ensure you an early seat on the Board.

The easy way will not work in all circumstances, however. For example:

- If you are female. (Marrying the boss's son does not have the same result. It will simply make you a fat cat's wife, and condemn you to a life of boring dinner parties, chairing charity committees and having to put up with a succession of mistresses.) In any case, women who want to become fat cats first have to break through something called the 'glass ceiling'. which is triple-glazed and reinforced with titanium.

- If the boss has no daughters.
- The boss has daughters but they are either already married or are impossibly ugly. (No aspiring fat cat can afford to have an ugly wife.)
- If you are gay – possible, but probably too risky unless you want a career in television.

The hard way
To win your way to the top in business and thus have the chance to become seriously rich you need three qualities:

- Above average intelligence. But not too far above – a PhD for example would be a grave handicap as clever people are looked upon with grave suspicion in the business community. If you are not too bright (or intellectually disadvantaged, to use the politically correct term) try the police or the army. If you are really gifted intellectually stay in the academic world.
- The ability to get on well with people. (The new buzzword is emotional intelligence). If your 'people skills' are poor, try the medical profession or the law.
- Ruthlessness. You will need the management

skills of Attila the Hun.

Years ago it was important to be heterosexual. Today it doesn't matter one way or the other if you are gay although unlike a career in politics it will not be a distinct advantage. It is, however, important to 'come out' early on and not wait to be 'outed' later in your career.

It is in the early stages of your career that the hard work is needed. Later on, once you are on the fast track for promotion, you will be carried on up the corporate hierarchy like a hot air balloon on a thermal.

From then on your career will benefit from the law of the self-fulfilling prophecy: if the boss thinks you have what it takes to get to the top he will prove his judgement correct by helping you get there. He will give you plum jobs and send you on expensive courses at top Business Schools, thus giving you a much better chance of making it than those who are not favoured with this 'crown prince' treatment.

Your first company
You should choose a business where you will be

likely to fit in well with the existing culture. For example, if you come from an upper middle class background and you have been educated at an expensive fee paying school and one of the older universities, then you are ideal material for an investment bank.

On the other hand, if your background is more plebeian, your accent provincial and you went to some obscure seat of higher education, you won't stand a chance of making it to the top in the world of high finance. Go instead for a company where an elitist background would be a distinct disadvantage. A solid engineering business with a provincial headquarters, for example.

Also, bear in mind that in companies which employ a lot of boffins or 'techies' there will not be a great deal of competition for advancement up the managerial ladder. Techies like to be left alone to get on with their technical work, and are only too grateful if someone else is willing to take on the job of managing the business, leaving them free to focus on their test tubes or software programmes.

If you are a woman your best chance of ending up at the top is to make your career in the world of investment banking or fund management. You might also stand a fair chance in an industry with a feminine association such as cosmetics or fashion but there are whole areas of industry that are a complete desert as far as women's careers are concerned, such as construction, civil engineering, the automotive industry, and chemicals.

Having the right accent is very important. Investment banking is a good choice for those with a Scottish accent since it is associated with prudence and integrity. In the USA a New England/Ivy league accent is best while in the UK a public school accent will get you far.

Make full use of any special skills you have. If for example you are a sporting type, go for a company which sponsors your particular sport – usually a clear indication of the chairman's interests. There are OK sports such as cricket and rugby in the UK and baseball and football in the US. Golf and tennis are acceptable everywhere, but keep quiet about any interest you take in snooker or pool. In the UK it is all right to be a supporter of one of the top soccer clubs such as Arsenal or Manchester United but not all right to confess to having played the game at school.

You may have picked up some special skills at school or college that made you popular but which are now best forgotten, such as waggling your ears or farting the National Anthem.

The fast track

Once you have joined the company you must focus on getting yourself onto the fast track for promotion. Some of the things you can do to make sure of this are:

Building your image

If you are male and want to become a top cat you should try to look and act the part;
This will involve investing in your appearance – smart well cut suits, expensive haircuts, top quality poplin shirts, and Italian silk ties. Shirts should have double cuffs that show a quarter of an inch below jacket sleeves. Shoes are particularly important.

The chairman may not notice you are wearing hand made shoes polished to a mirror-like finish, but his secretary will and that is just as important. Well manicured nails are also something she will notice, as well as your after shave lotion which should be expensive and applied with discretion.

Join a fitness club and work out regularly. Subscribe to the *Economist*, *Business Week*, the *Financial Times* and the *Wall Street Journal*.

If you are a woman remember that an aspiring female top cat would be wise not to go in for 'power dressing' too soon. The image to cultivate can be summed up in one word – immaculate. A smart well-cut suit in black or dark blue is recommended with a simple white or cream shirt and one small piece of jewellery. Skirts should be worn just above mid calf, nails perfectly manicured and finished with a plain lacquer. It goes without saying that you should spend a lot on your hair.

Keenness and commitment

Be one of the first to arrive at work, one of the last to leave; make a point of working late at least two evenings a week, making sure you are seen by any senior managers whom happen to be around. If you slip out for a beer use the well-known technique of leaving a jacket on the back of your chair.

Be bright eyed and bushy tailed at all times. Show a can-do attitude. Use phrases like 'no problem' or 'nothing is impossible' or 'the difficult can be done at once, the impossible may take a little longer'. Quote from self-improvement books such as *The Seven Habits of Highly Effective People* and leave copies of books like this lying around. Develop a bold, illegible, but instantly recognisable signature that conveys a sense of authority and inner strength.

Also read the latest management books or at least listen to the abridged versions on tapes when stuck in traffic jams. Use 'business-speak' with confidence. The main bits of jargon are listed below. Above all keep making the point that the overriding objective of business is to maximise shareholder value.

Management speak
The twenty top terms
Activity based costing

Balanced business scorecards
Benchmarking
Competitive advantage
Core competencies
Cost drivers
Downsizing
EBITDA (Earnings before interest, tax, deprecia-
tion and amortisation)
Emotional intelligence
EVA (economic vale added)
Human capital
Key success factors
Knowledge management
MVA (market value added)
Outsourcing
Partnership sourcing
Portfolio analysis
Strategic positioning
Synergy
Value chain

Get some good prints for your office (by fashionable modern artists such as Basquiat, Hockney,
Warhol or Tracy Emin).

Don't settle for a cheap modern car when for

MANAGEMENT SPEAK

the same money you can get a classic Cadillac, Mercedes or Jaguar.

Finally, remember that there are three kinds of people in a company – those that make things happen, those who watch things happen and those who ask 'What happened?' Make sure you are seen as one of the first kind.

The MBA

Ten years ago you could have got to the top without an MBA. Today it is more and more essential to have those magic three letters after your name. It is essential, however, that your MBA should come from one of the top accredited schools. The fees are very expensive so your best course of action is to try to get your company to sponsor you. If you have married the Chairman's daughter you stand a good chance of bringing this off but otherwise your best bet is to aim for a consultancy assignment to help pay the fees.

You may well learn a great deal from an MBA programme but very little of it will help you achieve your aim of becoming seriously rich. Indeed, if you take some of the subjects too seriously – business ethics for example – it could be counter productive.

The psychometric profile

From time to time you will probably be required to complete some kind of psychometric question-naire. These things are designed to measure your IQ and reveal your personality profile. In particu-lar the tests will be designed to assess your strengths and weaknesses in terms of your poten-tial as top management material.

Psychometric questionnaires in the work-place, unlike those in magazines, are not an opportunity to find out more about yourself, least of all an opportunity to confess your inner doubts and fears. Using your intelligence you should be able to work out which boxes to tick in order to come up with the kind of profile that will impress the people in Human Resources. They will be looking for traits associated with leadership qual-ities: extraversion, dominance, self-belief, deter-mination, ambition, flexibility, and creativity. They will pounce on any suggestion of introver-sion, rigidity of thinking or indecisiveness. It is a good idea to persuade a friendly psychologist to get you copies of the most frequently used tests so that you can practise picking the 'right' answers.

IQ tests can be trickier and it is more difficult to fudge the answers. Nevertheless, you can significantly increase your score by practising. There are plenty of books containing typical IQ test questions and doing these will enable you to become very familiar with the kinds of thought processes involved in answering them. The tests tend to be of three kinds, testing verbal, numerical and spatial intelligence. Find out where you are strong and weak, but remember that to get on in business verbal ability is more important than the others.

A useful rule is to try to work quickly. answering as many questions as possible in the time available, since with forced choice questions there is always a chance of getting a correct answer by chance.

The Assessment Centre

You may be required to spend a day or two at an Assessment Centre. If so, as well as filling in lots of questionnaires and taking various pencil and paper tests you will be interviewed more than once and invited to take part in a number of group exercises.

One type of interview is aimed at putting you under stress. Typically you will be asked a hypothetical question such as 'You are in a shipwreck; you are a powerful swimmer and can save one person. Close by and in danger of drowning are (a) A world famous heart surgeon. (b) a two year old child and (c) your wife's mother. Which would you save?' It does not matter in the slightest which one you choose; the interviewer will attack you mercilessly both on grounds of moral degeneracy and lack of clear logical thought. All you have to do is to defend your choice calmly and quietly. *The two ways to fail are to change your mind or to raise your voice.* (Mind you, these are often the causes of failing in real life!)

Another type of interview is the psychiatric one. It will help to read a popular book about psychoanalysis before taking this interview. It will give you some idea of what questions will be asked and what hang-ups the interviewer will be looking for. You will be asked about your childhood. Was it happy? What were your relationships with your parents and siblings like? Were you happy at school?

The best way to cope is to give positive answers to each question. Yes, you had an idyllically happy childhood; your schooldays were wonderfully happy; you really got on well with your siblings and still do; no you are not afraid of the dark, spiders or snakes; you do not have nightmares, you sleep soundly; your sex life is great; yes, of course you have masturbated and, no, you don't feel guilty about it.

When it comes to the group exercises, there are usually two kinds. In one type the leader is designated in advance. When it is your turn to act as group leader there are two things to remember. First, don't try to take decisions by yourself. Always involve the group members. This not only demonstrates a politically correct leadership style it happens also to be the best way of solving whatever problem has been set. Secondly, go out of your way to be considerate to any member from an ethnic minority and any no-hoper and, if you are male, to make sure any females in the group feel fully involved.

The other type of exercise involves a leaderless group. The observers will be watching to see how many leadership initiatives each member takes and how many are accepted by the rest of the group. To succeed in this situation you will need to have already established yourself as someone with leadership potential by having created the right image during the preceding stages of the Assessment Centre.

The people who emerge as leaders in such situations are the ones who are seen by their fellow group members as caring, concerned to maintain harmony in the group, protective of the weaker members and who very rarely use the 'I' word.

How you behave when the group is relaxing and not being observed is as important as or even more important than your behaviour during the exercises

Above all, never ever be heard to say anything negative about any other group member.

The performance review

In order to stay on the fast track you will need to

get an 'excellent' rating on each annual performance review. Your immediate superior will con-
duct the review so the first rule is always to keep
on very good terms with that person.

Lord Acton said that power corrupts; we all
know too well that money also corrupts, but
friendship can corrupt too and if your boss thinks
of you as a friend it will be very hard for him or
her to give you a bad report.

The second rule is to prepare well. List all
your accomplishments over the past year in great
detail, being careful to steer the narrow path
between embellishment and downright exagger-
ation. To give the appearance of balance, mention
a couple of instances where you failed to achieve
an objective, but make sure these instances relate
to relatively trivial matters.

Then comes the part where you list your
view of your development needs. Go for safe
things like improving your financial knowledge
or IT skills. To ask for more training and development in areas like interpersonal skills or assertive-
ness can be interpreted as a damaging admission
of weakness in these vital areas.

One more rule – thank your boss profusely

when the interview is over and say how very helpful you have found his or her advice and how much you have benefited from the coaching and mentoring you have received over the preceding twelve months.

Meetings

Nowadays, managers spend much of their time in meetings. These give you a great opportunity to shine.

The golden rule is 'Always wait to see which way the boss cat jumps before opening your mouth.'

Prepare well. Most people don't take the trouble to do more than glance through the relevant papers in advance of a meeting. Thorough preparation pays off. On key issues it is a good idea to prepare and circulate your own paper. This need not involve a lot of work. You can download a paper on almost any subject from the Internet – and the risk that anyone will rumble you is small.

If the meetings are scheduled for the early afternoon make sure you have a very light lunch, preferably a salad and above all no alcohol. You need to look and feel alert. Take notes, but don't doodle.

Get to the meeting in good time and choose your place with care. Make sure that you will be able to catch the chairman's eye easily and that your position is sufficiently central to enable you to address the other people at the meeting without getting 'Wimbledon neck' through having to keep looking in two different directions.

Under no circumstances ever be late for an important meeting. Rather than be late it is much better not to turn up at all, subsequently sending an apology and mentioning the dreadful accident you witnessed on the motorway that left you in a state of shock and caused your absence. (Whatever excuse you use, the outcome should be that people are very sympathetic towards you, that you are seen as the innocent victim of circumstances.)

When a meeting hots up and opinion becomes sharply divided on an important issue and angry exchanges start to take place, time is getting on and the chairman starts looking worried, it is time for you to intervene along the following lines:

'Chairman, I have listened carefully to both sides of this discussion and I think I know why it is that we are finding it so very difficult to reach agreement on a course of action.' (Here hold your audience by pausing for a moment or two until you have everyone's full attention.) 'Chairman, I think the reason we cannot agree is that we simply do not have enough information on which to base a sound decision. May I suggest, therefore, that we set up a small working party to investigate further and report back to the next meeting?' You then add that you would be quite willing to serve on such a working group. Now everyone will be happy. You have got the chairman off the hook and the protagonists of the various points of view can leave the meeting able to fight another day.

Your own meetings

When you are chairing a meeting remember there is only one test of whether a meeting has been a good one or a waste of time. *A good meeting is one where people walk away from it saying 'That was a good meeting'*. You can achieve this outcome if you remember that for most people the characteristics of a good meeting are:

- They have been given five minutes to air their particular hobbyhorse.
- The chairperson achieves consensus by the simple method of taking all the decisions.
- It lasts no more than an hour.

It is important to arrange for your secretary to interrupt if the meeting goes on longer and to say that there is an emergency that needs your urgent attention.

Presentations

Most young executives are terrified of having to make presentations, so this gives you a great opportunity to shine; get some coaching in presentation skills, become a whiz-kid with Power Point and lose no opportunity to show off your skill. Making first class presentations is one of the most highly prized skills in the world of business and will earn you countless brownie points.

Remember that slides containing lists of words are very boring. The whole point of a visual presentation is that there is something to look at – cartoons, graphs, photographs. Invest in your future. If it is a very important occasion pay a professional to prepare your presentation for you. Always use a laptop; under no circumstances ever make your presentation with a set of overhead foils. (On the other hand always have a set of overhead foils in reserve in case the technology fails.)

Finally, always remember to stop speaking before people stop listening.

Choosing your friends

Be friendly with your colleagues at work but save real friendship for others. In order to get on fast you will almost certainty need to trample on other people on the way and no one wants to do this to their real friends.

Associate with the 'in' crowd, the ones who are clearly favoured by top management. It is a good idea in the early years to pick out a fast rising star and cling to his tail. Steer clear of the ones who are going nowhere.

CHOOSING YOUR FRIENDS
You will almost certainly have to trample on
other people on the way

31

Social skills

Remember that in the business world, image and things like presence, self confidence and social skills are much more highly valued than qualifications. Here are some tips:

- Take up golf (but always know when to lose).
- Be attentive to the Chairman's wife at company functions.
- Always notice his secretary's new dress or hairstyle.
  (These last two are as important for women as for men.)
- Never appear to be the worse for drink. (It is, however, excusable to appear to be the better for drink, i.e. in the sense of being more relaxed, wittier.)
- Never go to a Thai or Indian restaurant at lunchtime.
- Prepare a few witty after dinner speeches and practise them. (There are plenty of books containing model speeches for all occasions.)
- Never tell sexist or racist jokes in public. Save them for your closest friends.
- Always be charming and friendly to people at

all levels of the company – you may need their support later on. Remember that there are no short people, just ones who are vertically challenged. Be politically correct at all times.

Some other things to remember:

- The purpose of a memorandum is not to convey information but to protect the writer.
- If you don't delegate you will have no one to blame when things go wrong.
- It is better to ask dumb questions than to make dumb mistakes.
- Don't try to become irreplaceable. People who can't be replaced seldom get recommended for promotion.
- Don't watch porn on the office computer.

If you follow all this advice carefully you will get your first chief executive job in your early thirties. However, don't spoil things by trying to get this far too quickly.

Remember it is better that people ask why you are <u>not</u> chief executive than that they ask why you <u>are</u>.

2. Winning the power game

Once you have got your first top cat CEO job you can make a start on a process which you can repeat with increasing finesse as you move on from company to company during your career. This is the vital one of *getting absolute control of the enterprise and its resources*, without which you won't be able to exploit your power to your maximum financial advantage.

The power structure
There are basically three types of arrangement at the top level of a company:

- An executive chairman together with a chief executive. In this situation the chairman is usually the most powerful figure. You should try to avoid companies with this structure.
- A non-executive, part-time chairman together

WINNING THE POWER GAME
The ultimate power position

with a chief executive. In this situation any chief executive worth his or her salt will quickly grasp the reins of power.

- The roles of chairman and chief executive are combined. This is the ultimate power position and the one you must aim for.

Controlling the Board

Let us assume that you get your first CEO job in a company with a non-executive chairman, one who is getting on in years and has many other commitments. Once you have won his or her confidence such a chairman will be only too willing to delegate a great deal to you.

The most important thing to concentrate on initially is to ensure that the other directors are fully supportive of you, which means that you must be able to select them and build your own team.

Choosing your finance director

This is the key appointment. The finance director must be very bright and technically very competent; you will need him to carry through some very sophisticated deals. It is, however, vitally important that of all the executive directors, the finance director should be absolutely loyal to you. The ideal candidate should be a well-qualified male, a timid introvert with a heavy mortgage, and three kids from his present marriage and two from his first marriage. You should pay him well above market rates and grant him generous stock options. He will be yours for life. Get him to keep changing the basis of the accounting system. As Robert Townshend pointed out in *Up the Organisation*, this is the best way to do a 'snow job' on the accounts.

The other executive directors

As for the other executive directors, you will be wise to select for mediocrity so that your own star will shine the more brightly.

Ideally one of them (preferably the Human Resource Director) should be a woman as evidence of your progressive approach. If she comes from an ethnic minority, better still.

Again, generous reward packages will help

ensure their loyalty to you personally. But remember – titles cost nothing.

From time to time you should fire one of the executive directors. It helps keep the others on their toes.

Combining both roles

Given a compliant team of executives and a non executive chairman at the end of his career, you must work towards the day when, on the chairman's retirement, you are able to persuade the board that it is a good idea to appoint you Chairman as well as Chief Executive. This done, you can then set about changing the rest of the non-executives. Board arguments are most distasteful and should be avoided at all costs; your aim should be to ensure that your Board is characterised by harmony and consensus.

Selecting the non-executives

The ideal profile for a non-executive director is any of the following:

- Pillars of rectitude. Look for people whose reputations are beyond reproach and who, because of their titles, honours, or membership of professional bodies will give the board as a whole an image of integrity.
- Well-connected people who can get you into the right clubs, introduce you into desirable social circles, and help with hosting VIP entertainment.
- Little or no business knowledge or experience. You don't want people who can challenge the way you are runnng the company.
- Needy – in other words people who depend on their directors' fees to maintain their lifestyles. People who have been hit by some bad investments are a good source, especially those paying alimony.

Those who meet the bill include retired naval officers, preferably Admirals, retired government officials, business school professors, and in the UK, members of the House of Lords (on the whole impoverished hereditary peers are likely to have better connections than life peers).

You will, however, need at least one leading

businessman on your Board, on the understand-
ing that you in turn will be invited to serve as a
non-executive on his Board. If you then sit on
each other's Remuneration Committee you will
be able to put into practice that well-known fat
cat philosophy 'You scratch my back and I'll
scratch yours'.

The organisation structure

There are a number of principles to bear in mind
when deciding on the organisation structure of
the business.

The first is Divide and Rule. A functional
structure based on Finance, Sales and Operations
will lead to a great deal of infighting and struggling for power, taking the pressure off you.

The second is delayering. Managerial salaries
are expensive. Employ as few as possible. As well
as saving money the organisation will almost certainly become more efficient.

The third is the time-honoured principle of
Unity of Command – which means the boss takes
all the decisions.

The symbols of power

As exemplified by Hitler and the Wizard of Oz, the exercise of power is greatly enhanced by the clever manipulation of symbols.

Among these the most important is the Chairman's office. This has two aspects, the physical and the human.

The physical office should be large, that goes without saying. It should be furnished more like a living room than a workspace. You should sit at a table rather than a desk. When receiving visitors you should invite them to join you in the sitting area. The carpet should be very, very deep. Lots of fresh flowers, well chosen pictures (always originals or at the very least, signed limited edition prints.) The furnishing should either be genuine antique (never reproduction) or ultra modern steel and beechwood. Lighting is terribly important; as people enter the room the bright lights should hit their eyes and dazzle them, while you are bathed in the soft light of a single desk lamp.

Between your office and the rest of the head office building there should be a long, luxuriously carpeted corridor and two outer offices one for your PA and one for his or her private secretary.

THE SYMBOLS OF POWER
The Dragon at the entrance of the cave

As for the human side, the most important aspect is the 'dragon at the entrance to the cave'. In other words, you're personal assistant or PA. The best choice is a woman of mature years and great presence. Her job is to manage your diary, prevent people from gaining access to you and wasting your valuable time. Establish a set of rules, such as no employee seeking an appointment with you will be given one less than three weeks ahead. When people do turn up to keep their appointments with you, make sure they are kept waiting for at least ten minutes before being admitted. The dragon's job includes reminding you of your next appointment once each employee has had his or her ten minutes of your valuable time.

• The second most important symbol of power at this stage of your career is your choice of car (the corporate jet comes later.) Always have the current model. Be chauffeur driven as often as possible. It is better to have at least two cars – if you are working in Britain use a Jaguar (ignoring the fact that it is owned by Ford) and a

BMW or Mercedes if you are doing business with the Germans. In the US you will need a whole fleet.

Winning over the investment community

The aim here is to become known in financial circles as someone who is rising rapidly in the business world, a sound strategist, unequivocally committed to maximising shareholder value, and yet at the same time progressive and socially responsible.

- The first step is to appoint a PR Agency. In the early years go for a small but highly creative boutique – one which will really need your fees. Make it plain to them that their main task is to boost your personal image.
- Employ corporate identity consultants to give your company a fresh image. Key themes are 'dynamic growth', 'market focus', 'globally competitive', 'world class environmentally friendly' and 'high-tech.' Get them to come up with a new name that expresses these ideas. Follow the outstanding examples of the recent past such as Accenture, Monday and Diageo.

- Develop a clear business strategy. This involves two steps. First, hire McKinsey or some other top-flight consultancy to work it out for you. Second, convene a strategy conference involving all your senior executives and hold it in superb surroundings with a world class golf course – somewhere like Hilton Head Island in Georgia. Hire in a top class media firm to devise a dramatic multimedia presentation followed by fireworks. This should ensure 'buy in'.

- Make speeches on every possible occasion in which you constantly stress that the job of the chief executive is to focus exclusively on creating total shareholder value. Build a reputation as a leading spokesperson for the free market. You will find it best to employ a speechwriter for this.

- Spend freely on the company's Annual Report. Use a top design team. Ensure that the report carries several pictures of you in different contexts – with employees, with customers, involved in community affairs, etc. Use the report to set out a clear statement of strategic intent backed by statements of Vision, Mission and Values. (You can get the team at the PR Agency to draft these for you.) Make sure it

contains all the right messages about people
("Our greatest asset," etc.), sustainable development and the environment.

Getting the auditors on your side

In every aspect of business life personal relationships count for a great deal. A prudent Chairman
and Chief Executive will establish close relationships with the firm's auditors.

* Choose an audit firm in the middle size range
  one that will be glad of the fee income, but large
  enough to be beyond reproach.
* Get to know the senior partners well – include
  them in your top-level corporate entertainment
  programme.
* Don't ignore the juniors who will actually carry
  out the work on site. Go out of your way to
  welcome them and invite them to the less prestigious or less popular company events – sponsored classical music concerts, for example.
* The Board's Audit Committee should ideally
  consist of yourself and two of your carefully
  selected non-executives.

A cautionary note

Once you are chairman of a reasonably sized plc take great care over your public utterances. The kinds of things to avoid saying include the following slips of the tongue from past AGM's:

'This is the worst disaster to happen to this company since I was appointed chairman.'

'We are having an average year – worse than last year, but better than next year is going to be.'

'Forecasting is very difficult, especially in relation to the future'.

'I know the recession is over. Our salesmen are beginning to lose bigger orders.'

Don't worry about being popular. Be like the chairman who, when taken to hospital following a slight heart attack, received the following message from fellow directors: 'The Board wishes you a speedy recovery. This motion was carried by five votes to four.'

3. Joining the 'Great and the Good'

The aim in this next step of your journey is to build for yourself a reputation as a macho, charismatic world class business leader, somebody who 'makes a difference'. So, as you move on from one company to another there are some basic steps that you must take at each stage.

Becoming a transformational leader

On taking up each new appointment the first thing to do is to institute a radical profit improvement campaign.

This will involve taking the kind of steps that most chief executives need to take from time to time as economic conditions change. These short term measures can, however, damage the health of the business and fine judgement is called for in balancing survival in the short term against the sustainability of the business in the longer term.

This should not worry you, however, since, as an aspiring fat cat, you will have moved on to your next, larger company well before any long term negative effects become apparent.

The following are the essential elements of your strategy:

- Reduce the numbers employed at Head Office drastically. Sell off the Head Office premises and move the survivors to a suburban or provincial location where rent, rates and wage and salary levels are lower. (But keep a small private office with a flat above for yourself in Mayfair or Manhattan).
- Hire consultants to carry out a thorough restructuring of the rest of the organisation. *Brief them carefully as to what you expect their findings to be.*
- Outsource all non-core activities.
- Reduce the number of plants/branches/outlets.
- Dispose of all surplus land and property.
- If the company is in manufacturing, introduce Japanese methods such as Just in Time, thus

reducing inventory drastically.

- Reduce the number of employees, but do so by the most economical methods – early retirement, and a freeze on recruiting, avoiding large redundancy payments. This approach will also help build your reputation as a caring employer.
- Cut the budgets for capital expenditure, research and development and training.
- Move as many activities as possible offshore to countries with lower labour costs. IT staff are available at cheap rates in India. If your company is in manufacturing, relocate as much production as possible to Eastern Europe or the Far East.
- Close the company's final salary pension scheme and substitute a defined contribution scheme for all new employees. If there is a surplus in the old pension fund take the opportunity to take a contributions 'holiday'.
- Go all out for as many business awards as possible (EFQM, Baldrige, ISO 9000, ISO 14001, in the UK the Queen's Award for Exports and/or Technology, etc.)
- Review all insurance premium costs including

those for health cover for employees and their dependants and for permanent disability.

Once these actions are showing results invite a prominent Business School professor to write a case study on how you achieved such a transformation in performance. Make sure your PR Company gets the story well covered in the Press; accept invitations to tell the story at prestigious business conferences. Then watch the stock out-perform the index.

Having achieved success of this kind in a company with a turnover of £50 million or $100m, move on and repeat it in a company turning over £100 million or $250m. Carry on, moving every two to three years. Each time you do this your reputation will grow and head-hunters offering you your next job will pursue you. Never forget to move on before the story becomes stale and, above all, before any problems develop.

Networking

In the process of growing your reputation, networking in the wider business environment should supplement what you are doing inside the business. Here are some of the more obvious ploys.

- Become active in regional branches of the top business leaders associations in the early years, paving the way for serving on National Committees of these bodies later in your career.
- Similarly, become active in your industry's trade association. Represent it when lobbying for government support. If it is a prestigious association your long-term aim should be to become its President.
- Entertain lavishly in all the right places – In the UK the important ones are Henley, Wimbledon, Ascot, the British Open, etc. In America the US Open and the Rosebowl are essential. Try to choose events to which you can invite people to be accompanied by their spouses or partners – this will win you a lot of friends.
- Hold regular lunches to which you invite business journalists, prominent businessmen, investment analysts and other opinion formers. Starting modestly with local press representa-

THE SECOND SPOUSE
Try to arrange a quiet amicable divorce

tives and your local politicians you can work up to inviting top politicians and people like the Editor of the *Economist* or the *Wall Street Journal* in the later years. Hold these lunches in most exclusive restaurants.

- With the aid of your non-executive directors obtain membership in one or two good clubs.
- Get on the list of those invited to Davos every year and mingle with world leaders. (Davos is the Swiss ski resort, which is the venue for the annual meeting of the World Economic Forum. Every winter since 1971 around 2,000 of the world's business, political and scientific elite meet for an intense six-day bout of conference speeches, private meetings and quiet dinners.)

The second spouse

As your reputation and social standing grow it is more and more important that you should have a partner who can add lustre to social occasions. If you married young, you probably did not choose your husband or wife in terms of suitability to be the spouse of a top business leader in later years. At some stage you will have to remedy this situation.

If you are a man, the kind of wife to charm the people you need to influence almost certainly needs to be younger and more beautiful than your present wife. So you should try and arrange a quiet, amicable divorce – you can afford it by now. Find for yourself a second wife who can symbolise your success and standing. Look for a well-educated, very good-looking young woman in her late twenties/early thirties, preferably a natural blonde. She should come from a good family background, and be an accomplished dinner party hostess and conversationalist. Invite her to take her place alongside you as the chairman's wife – having first shown her the company flat in town, the company yacht, your platinum corporate credit card and others of your charms.

If you are a woman it is important not to be embarrassed in any way by your husband's presence on important occasions. The worst thing that can happen is to have to be accompanied by a gin-sodden nonentity when meeting the good and the great. You need a husband who, while not outshining you and your achievements, commands respect for his own place in the world. Ideally a consultant surgeon, a successful writer, an architect of distinction. If your first husband doesn't match up, get rid of him.

Corporate Social responsibility

It is increasingly important in relations with the investment community that your business should be seen to be socially responsible. This boils down to two main things – being seen to be concerned about the environment and acting in such a way as to benefit the local communities in areas where the company has operations. To be seen to be socially responsible involves making politically correct statements and giving out all the right messages. It also helps to win a few awards. The best ones to go for are things like the award for the best annual report incorporating some form of social and environmental audit. This type of award is given not so much for what you do but for what you say about it, which makes it easier for your PR company to get you at least onto the short list.

It is important to sponsor events in local communities, particularly ones to do with schools. These need add little to costs and help divert attention from difficult issues such as how much atmospheric or water pollution results from your firm's activities. Make sure your notepaper, packaging materials and publications carry the message 'manufactured from recycled materials'.

Good works

A rounded reputation as a progressive business-man in today's society calls for a track record of public service There are some basic requirements under this heading.

- Become chairman of a charity, preferably one to do with animals. This should not take up too much of your time. It is a good idea to start by firing the incumbent director, using head-hunters to find a successor and then leaving him or her to get on with running things.
- Make significant donations to charitable causes or, rather, persuade the Board that the company should do so.
- Sponsor one or two activities – one cultural and one sporting. These should be chosen with care so as to give you the maximum publicity for the

money. Your PR company should try to ensure that these sponsorships are linked with your name as much as with the company's.

- Make a donation to a University Business School.

As your career develops, the scale and scope of these activities can grow. The ultimate goal should be to become chairman of a National Charity dealing with a popular cause, to fund a named Chair at a prestigious business school, to sponsor one of the country's cultural icons, and to back a championship winner in the field of sport.

Assuming you also persuade the company to contribute generously to the ruling political party, activities such as these should establish you as one of the good and the great before you are 40. When you finally get headhunted to be chairman and chief executive of a FTSE 100 or Fortune 500 company, two or three honorary doctorates and the odd gold medal will follow.

Your biographical details

Around this time you will be invited to submit an

entry into such reference books as *The International Who's Who*, the *Dictionary of International Biography* or *Top People of Today*. In preparing your entry you can be economical with the truth, but do avoid outright fabrications. By all means exaggerate your achievements but don't actually make any up. They could come back to haunt you in later years. (An example of a creative entry, assuming you have attended a short business course at the Harvard Business School at some point, is to enter Harvard University after the name of your own university under the heading 'educated at...')

4. Life as a Top Cat

Choosing your company

Now that you have become a really top cat it is time to do two things. The first – the subject of this chapter – is to ensure that you now enjoy the rewards you richly deserve as a result of all your hard work and persistence. The second, which will be covered in the next chapter, is to prepare your exit strategy and guarantee your golden parachute.

If you have followed the steps described in the previous chapters you will by now be approached by several prominent firms of head-hunters to take on the role of chief executive of a really major company. You must choose among these offers with great care.

The key criteria are:

• The company should be in the FTSE100 or Fortune 500. (If you are British a FTSE100 company is essential if you are to get your knighthood. Failure to achieve this would be very disappointing for your wife for whom becoming a titled lady has been an enduring ambition.)

- The job should combine the roles of chairman and chief executive. (You don't want some elderly member of the business establishment looking over your shoulder and questioning your decisions.)

- The company must be London or New York based. You cannot achieve your ambitions in a company based in the Provinces.

- The business should not be in bad shape. You are not aspiring to be a company doctor or a turnaround specialist. It should ideally be a well-established business that has been performing very satisfactorily and that has acquired a certain amount of fat as a consequence. You want to be able to take advantage of some low hanging fruit to make quick, dramatic savings when you take over.

- The business should have some hidden assets, such as relatively unprofitable operations being carried out on potentially highly valuable sites.

The remuneration package

Once you have chosen you can begin negotiating the all-important remuneration package. This involves six elements: the service contract, salary and bonus, share options, pension arrangements and 'perks'. (Just as there is more than one way to skin a cat, but there is more than one way of fattening it up.)

The service contract

You should aim at a five-year service contract. Since the game plan will mean your staying no longer than three years this will enable you in due course to claim compensation for loss of office. Make sure that it includes generous compensation arrangements in case of loss of office due to a merger or acquisition (a change of control clause). This is vital step in ensuring your golden parachute.

Salary

Your salary may well be the least significant of your financial rewards, but it is important as it establishes your position in the league table of top executives. A good guide to the salary you should demand is the going rate in other FTSE or Fortune 500 companies. The current benchmark in the UK, where, relative to the US, executive salaries are relatively modest, is a minimum multiple of 50 times the salary of the average employee. Assuming the average employee in the company of your choice is earning £20,000 a year this would set your salary at £1 million. You may well be able to negotiate a higher figure than this. In the US salaries vary a lot. Robert Murdoch's salary in the year 2000 was $4,350,000 yet Carly Fiorina, chief executive of Hewlett Packard earned a modest $1,248,073 in 2001.

You should insist on the inclusion of a bonus scheme that should enable you to at least double your earnings in a single year. The criteria for the award of bonus should be linked to short term increases in the company's share price, as this is what you are going to spend your time boosting. As to what to aim for, well, Michael Eisner of Disney earned $8,500,000 in bonus in the year 2000.

Share options
It follows that you should also negotiate the best possible share option arrangement, one that is

triggered by relatively modest increases in earnings per share. (Earnings growth will make you very popular in the financial districts, although it tells investors nothing about the more important measure of return on capital employed. You will not find it difficult to grow earnings rapidly while returns fall, simply by increasing the capital base through acquisitions.) Take full advantage of any schemes that will enable you to make tax free capital gains – your lawyers and tax advisers will know all about these. Eisner gained $63,500,000 through share options in the year 2000.

Pension arrangements
Although you only plan to spend three years with the company this is no reason why you should not hold out for generous pension arrangements. (A useful benchmark here is Percy Barnevik who retired from his post as chairman of ABB with a £61 million pension – although he did have to apologise and give £37 million back after pressure from the Swedish investment company Investor. Another indicator is the annual pension fund contribution of £990,000 in the case of the CEO of Barclays).

Perks

This is where the finer points of negotiating come in. Your shopping list should include:

- An executive jet aircraft at your disposal.
- Use of a company flat in Mayfair or Manhattan (preferably both).
- VIP status at Heathrow.
- Chauffeur driven top of the range car, including collection from and return to home.
- Platinum corporate credit card.

Other perks such as seats at the Royal Opera House or the Metropolitan can be arranged once you have taken the reins of power.

You should, of course, be sensitive to the possibility of adverse comment on all this by the press or by some of the investment institutions or pension funds. It is important at this stage to avoid attracting the label 'fat cat'. You can guard against this by ensuring that possible criticism is silenced by your early success in raising the share price.

Live well but keep fit. A man can allow his waist line to expand with dignity just as his hairline may recede a little, but only to the extent that is consistent with his growing eminence. A little greying at the temples, natural or otherwise can help promote the elder statesman look at this stage. It will also help if, when you are seen in public or are photographed for the press that you appear informal, relaxed and casual. Try wearing open necked shirts, be photographed playing handball with some of the rank and file employees, make it known that you prefer a beer to brandy or champagne.

As always, it is going to be more difficult if you are a woman. Staying slim and good-looking is a must, so budget for regular botoxin injections and possibly cosmetic surgery. Take Margaret Thatcher, during her Premiership, as a role model. If you can look like that you will have no problems. On formal occasions dress simply, with minimum jewellery. For work there is no alternative to the well cut suit and blouse.

The Board

At this level your board will be subject to close scrutiny by the institutions for its conformity with the latest recommendations for the reform of corporate governance. In order to be seen as whiter than white your board should pass the following tests, *none of which will act as a constraint on you doing exactly what you want to do:*

- You should publish the terms of the executive directors' contracts.
- The majority of executives should be non-executive. One of these should be nominated as the senior non-executive director.
- You should publish the membership of the remuneration, nomination and audit committees, each of which should be chaired by a senior non-executive director.
- Share options should be conditional upon achieving performance standards.

You must select your non-executives with care, as you very much need them to be on your side. As senior non-executive director and chairman of the remuneration committee you should appoint the chairman of another FTSE100 or Fortune 500 company – someone with whom you have developed good relations in past years.

An equally respected figure – this time from the City or Wall Street – should be invited to chair the audit committee. Otherwise all you will need is an ex ambassador or permanent secretary together with the expected female director.

How to enjoy it

It is of no use having all this if you don't have time to enjoy it.

It should take only the first three months after taking over control of the business to set in motion all those actions designed to raise profits and which were listed in the previous chapter. You are by now well practised in such processes as downsizing, outsourcing, closing the head office, cutting the budgets for R. and D. and capital expenditure, reducing inventory, re-engineering and moving production offshore. The executive directors, reinforced with an army of consultants, can then be left to get on with implementation and you can begin to relax with the secure knowledge that, by the third quarter, dramatic profit growth will fuel a sharp rise in the share value. If there is some criticism of your approach you can quote Jack Welch who famously said when he took charge at GE 'I didn't start with a morale problem, I created it'.

The scene is now set for the good times to begin – always, of course set in the context of customer entertainment and supporting worthy causes. Formula One races, Glyndebourne, The Cannes Film Festival. Goodwood and Ascot. The Rosebowl, The US Open, The Ryder Cup, all these and more can now be built into your schedule.

The key to success at this stage is to enjoy the fruits of success to the greatest possible extent while at the same tme reinforcing your reputation as a caring, responsible business leader as well as a conspicuously successful one.

Here are some ideas.

• When using the company jet to visit overseas subsidiaries, try to combine the trip with an activity that can be featured in the press as demonstrating your concern for the environment or human rights. For example when visiting your company in Brazil by all means take a break in Rio but also take the opportunity to be pictured meeting a group of people campaigning for the preservation of the rain forests. Better still, follow the example of Ken Lay when he was chairman of ENRO and send the jet on medical emergency missions when you have no need of it.

- On any trip to Africa combine a safari park holiday with (for instance) presenting a company sponsored ambulance to an impoverished local community and be photographed with a crowd of smiling black children.

Playing away from home

If you are male a mistress is essential to your image as a macho business leader. You will have no trouble getting one. Power is a very strong aphrodisiac and you will be able to pick and choose among the fairest in the land. You should choose carefully. Try to find a married lady – preferably titled or the wife of a senior politician or top rank government official. She will have as much reason as you will to be discreet. Also, given her own domestic and social commitments she won't take up too much of your time.

Moreover as you will not need to set her up in a separate Mayfair flat she will be quite economic.

If you are female you may from time to time wish to enjoy the company of a young male escort, but there is no need to make other than financial arrangements for this purpose.

For UK eyes only – Getting your K

As well as enjoying the rewards of success you can concentrate on a key life goal – getting your knighthood or becoming a Dame. As Chairman of a FTSE100 company you are halfway there. To complete your qualification you will need to do some of the following:

- Win a Business in the Community Award.
- Make a substantial contribution to the funds of the Party in government.
- Chair a task force to improve the efficiency of the NHS or the railways, or to find ways of reducing the level of crime.
- Get elected President of the Confederation of British Industry.

- Become Chairman of a major national charity or Arts body.
- Employ the best possible PR agent. (This one is essential).

Now that your financial and social ambitions are well on the way to being realised it is time to turn your attention to planning your exit strategy. This will be the subject of the next chapter.

5. The golden parachute

You are now about to follow a well-trodden path – one that leads to a huge cash payoff and financial security for the rest of your life – the path to your golden parachute. You must not at any stage let yourself be diverted from the single-minded pursuit of your goal – to make yourself seriously rich.

In the process you will do nothing illegal. You will not need to. Accepted practices in the financial markets and associated regulations are quite flexible enough to accommodate your aims.

From start to finish this should take between three and five years depending on market conditions. Your strategy involves four stages.

Stage 1 Boost earnings and share price

The first steps have already been described in the previous chapter – improving short-term earnings

THE GOLDEN PARACHUTE

and giving the share price a hefty boost. You will be giving the institutions what they most desire – growth.

Stage 2 The big acquisition

By now the institutions will be expecting you to make your first really big acquisition. The investment banks and big corporate law firms in particular will be sniffing around for custom. Make sure that it is well understood that an investment bank that strongly recommends your own company's stock will be a strong candidate for the job. You should confine your 'beauty parade' to the top companies such as Merrill Lynch, Morgan Stanley Dean Witter, Goldman Sachs, CSFB, or J P Morgan.

Make sure you can present a strong case for the acquisition. Start using phrases like economies of scale, synergistic integration, market leadership and global compass.

Don't be put off by studies such as that by KPMG in 2001 that showed that only 30 percent of the 1997-1999 mergers studied created value, while nearly 40 percent produced no difference and 31 percent destroyed value. Nor McKinsey & Co's findings that 61 percent of acquisitions were failures in terms of rate of return to investors.

No one else apart from business school academics takes any notice of such surveys, so why should you? If shareholders challenge you, give reply 'What is the cost of *not* making an acquisition'?

From the viewpoint of your objectives there are three main reasons for making a big acquisition at this stage.

- First, you will end up with a much bigger company, hence a much bigger salary, and an even more prominent position in the world of business.
- Second, it will give you yet another opportunity for downsizing, rationalisation and cost cutting, thus further boosting your reputation as a tough, macho business leader.
- Finally, although in the end it will almost inevitably start to go wrong, in the meantime your stock options will increase in value.

You can choose between two ways of financing the acquisition. One is by borrowing the necessary cash from the banks thus increasing the company's debt burden. This way does mean you will have to convince the banks that the deal makes sense. With your track record this should not be too difficult. Your PR agency will, of course, be feeding the financial press with stories explaining the virtues of the transaction.

The easier way is to offer the shareholders of the company to be acquired stock in your own company. This dilutes the holdings of your existing shareholders and usually involves paying a higher price than would be the case in a cash deal.

The best method from the point of view of your game plan is probably to offer stock, particularly as you know to what extent your company's stock is over-valued. In this way, too, you will avoid bank covenants that are unduly restrictive.

Your target company should be one whose directors will almost certainly oppose the merger. This will give you an opportunity to fight and win a glorious take-over battle, thus adding still further to your macho image and making you even more popular among the firms of merchant bankers, lawyers, PR agents, etc. whose coffers will be enriched by the extra fees that a contested bid gives rise to.

Having successfully brought off the acquisition and fired the whole top team from the acquired business you now call in another army of consultants. Their brief will be to maximise short-term cost savings through a process euphemistically known as rationalisation. This consists of yet more staff reductions across the board, plant closures, disposal of surplus land and buildings, and a squeeze on suppliers. Within six months you can issue a press release stating how many millions of pounds worth of costs have been saved as a result of your shrewd business move.

By now, if your PR agency has been doing its job your shares should be trading at a considerable premium to their intrinsic value in terms of long term cash flows. This is entirely due to you – not only because of what you have done to cut costs and raise profitability, but also because you are personally someone in whom shareholders, the institutions and the financial press have enormous confidence and trust. Confidence is the strongest currency of all in the markets and you are now going to cash in on it.

Stage 3

At first, in the stage of post-acquisition euphoria, the merged company's share price will continue to rise. But as the inevitable problems associated with the bedding in of a new acquisition begin to bite, earnings will begin to decline and ultimately the share price will follow. At first the decline in market capitalisation will be gradual. This gives you time to make your next move and you can extend this period of grace through good PR. Explain the drop in earnings as a temporary blip due to the time it takes for a major acquisition to begin to show the benefits of synergy and the economies of scale. There will be other excuses you can draw upon – unfavourable currency movements or such pernicious governmental impositions on enterprise as minimum wage legislation.

Stage 4

It is now time to begin the process that will lead to your pulling the ripcord on your golden parachute. You need to arrange for your company to be acquired in turn, preferably by a large, prestigious US based multinational that will be prepared to pay cash for it. A US acquirer is vital, since compensation payments that are seen as highly generous in the UK or Europe will seem very modest by US standards. It is important to find a cash buyer since that is most likely to produce an immediate uplift to your share price.

It is important to lay the ground for this by ensuring that you and your company are known in all three major financial centres. You can play your part by giving US, European and Japanese fund managers personal briefings, usually at attractive venues like Las Vegas, Monte Carlo or Bermuda. Your PR company's job is to get adulatory articles about you in *Fortune*, *Business Week*, the *Economist* and other influential business media and to arrange for you to appear on some business related TV programmes. You may not become as well known internationally as people like Percy Barnevik, Richard Branson or Jack Welch, but you can learn a lot from the way they set about it.

You will then be welcomed when you set up meetings with the chairmen and CEOs of potential acquirers. It is a good idea to see if you can get an auction going. The higher the price you get, the higher the value of your shareholding and the more pleased will your shareholders be. Also, an auction is a competitive situation and macho business leaders like to win. The urge to win can overcome the need for protracted due diligence. (We all know what it is like when we fall in love with a house and there are other bidders; who can be bothered with a full survey in such a situation?)

Make it clear that you do not expect to be retained by the acquirer who, in any case will almost certainly want to put their own man in control. At the same time also make it clear that you will expect generous compensation.

When it comes down to negotiating your package let your lawyers act for you. What should you ask for? The answer depends on where you are located. At the extreme for a UK based company is the benchmark pay-off by music group EMI who paid Jim Fifield £6.27 million for the early termination of his contract along with a retirement contribution of £6.15 million when he resigned from the EMI board and as president and chief executive officer of its US subsidiary EMI music in the late 1990s. This did, however, reflect US rather than UK practice. In the UK Derek Wanless left his job as chief executive of NatWest bank in October 1999, after the once-mighty bank fell prey to a number of hostile take-over attempts from much smaller firms. He received a pay-off worth a reported £3m, one of the biggest golden parachutes ever seen in the UK up to that time. Golden handshakes of more than £1 million are now commonplace. Payments of that order were made to a record 14 senior executives in the UK last year. Top of the list was a £9.1 million retirement gift to Klaus Esser, after Vodafone took over German telecoms group Mannesmann.

In second place was Jim Mueller, who presided over 14,000 job cuts (or to put it in euphemistic business jargon, rationalised the workforce) when a City merger created Invensys, the troubled automation group. He left his post with a £3.2 million handshake.

The acquiring company will, of course, be getting a company that is by now anorexic. Understaffed in relation to its workload, losing some of its most talented employees in consequence; under-invested in plant and equipment and in research. But it will take another year or two before all this neglect of fundamentals comes home to roost. In the meantime you will be stepping down at the peak of your reputation, leaving behind a company with an historically high market capitalisation whose shares are trading at a huge premium to the business's underlying worth. If your lawyers have done their job you will be leaving with a substantial seven figure cash sum and an extremely generous pension plan. If you have stuck to your plan throughout and made all the right moves at the right time you will have achieved all this by the time you are in your mid-fifties.

The stage is then set for the golden twilight of your career. There are now so many new ways open to you by which you can increase your wealth further without ever again having to work hard and these will be described in the next chapter.

6. The golden twilight

The big decision

Congratulations! You have succeeded in retiring with your reputation intact and your bank account greatly enlarged.

You now have two alternatives to choose between. On the one hand you can afford to sit back and enjoy life and do all the things you want to, with unlimited time on your hands. Or you can exploit your reputation and make a lot more money before you finally sign off. Assuming you are now in your late 50's or early 60's you have a decade or so ahead in which you can grow even richer and do so without incurring the stress of real responsibility. Which will you choose? The answer is obvious. A fat cat will never turn away from the chance to get richer any more than a domestic cat will spurn a plate of freshly chopped liver.

THE GOLDEN TWILIGHT

The 100 days

First you must decide how many days a year you want to spend working. All cool cats like to play and you must not give up too much of your leisure time. Given that there are about 240 days in the year on which you could work if you wished, and that you will need at least 40 for holidays there are 200 available. Why not work for half of these? You then need to work out how to maximise your earnings from 100 days. Here are the possibilities:

Non-executive directorships

An appointment as non-executive chairman for a major company might earn you £500,000 a year in the UK, more in the USA, plus perks, but you would need to give the company something like 30 days a year of your time and be available at other times. To be 'on call' might intrude too much on your enjoyment of life. Also, bearing in mind some recent problems such as Marconi or Enron, why risk putting your reputation on the line in a situation in which as a non-executive chairman you clearly would not have control?

On the other hand each non-executive directorship on the board of a smaller company could bring in a tidy sum and you would need only attend board meetings say nine a year at the most, usually taking up a half day. Less prestigious, perhaps, but making good economic sense. You could take on four or five of these, bringing in around half a million a year plus expenses.

Playing the non-executive game

Playing the part of an effective non-executive director need not demand too much energy or time. The way to cope is to have a small private office in a fashionable business district, tax deductible of course, and to employ as your PA a young woman with an MBA degree specialising in finance. Her job will be to keep your diary and to go through all the board papers of the companies whose boards you sit on and, in advance of each meeting. Before each meeting she will supply you with one sheet of paper containing a summary of the company's trading position and key financials, plus three searching questions to put to the exccutives.

Your job is simply to turn up at each meeting, put your prepared questions, speak in support of the Chairman at the AGM and constantly congratulate the executive team on doing a fine job in difficult trading conditions. Three things to remember:

- Never get confused as to which company's board meeting you are at on any one occasion.
- Don't try to do two board meetings in the same day.
- Make sure you are fully insured (and that the company pays the premium).

The masterstroke

The main plank of your post retirement strategy, however, should be to become a:

Celebrity

Although you have shown how it is possible to

get seriously rich in business you also know that the really rich people in today's society are the **celebrities**.

Look at it this way – a top business executive can earn in the region of £25,000 a week, but a celebrity can earn as much for a single personal appearance. So why not join them?

The first and essential step is to get a good start. Personal recommendation is vital here. Bear in mind that there are several levels in the celebrity hierarchy:

International, world class celebrities – Nelson Mandela, former Presidents of the United States (with one or two notable exceptions), David Beckham, Joan Collins, Margaret Thatcher, Tiger Woods and the like.

International celebrities, but short of legendary quality such as the Duchess of York, Tom Hanks, Pete Sampras, Richard Branson, J K Rowling or George Soros.

National celebrities – famous at home but unknown overseas like most contemporary British pop groups.

Minor celebrities – the sorts of people who open department stores or supermarkets or take part in gameshows on TV.

Complete non-entities who are struggling to become minor celebrities and who open charity shops.

Make sure you are on the books of an agent who represents someone in the first group. As in business, you must aim for the top and use every trick in the book to get there.

Some of the routes to celebrity status are the following:

The book

If this sounds too much like hard work remember you don't actually have to write it, just chat to a ghostwriter as you sit by the pool sipping Martinis. Hire a good agent and start an auction for the rights. (At a recent literary award ceremony one celebrity said he was glad to be present and thus have the opportunity of meeting the person who wrote his autobiography).

Writing your memoirs will not only make some useful additional cash, it will enable you to do two other things that can be immensely satisfying.

- Polish your own image to an even greater brilliance as you describe your masterstrokes of business strategy.
- Rubbish the careers and reputations of any people who have stood in your way in the past.

The TV series

You could try to follow the example of UK's John Harvey Jones and make a TV series. His *TroubleShooter* was tremendously successful and the videos sold thousands. You would need to find a different formula from the company doctor role. One possibility is a series on great business leaders of today which should earn you a few more powerful friends as well as a great deal of cash. Another book can then follow based on the series.

The lecture circuit

Using the same agent, solicit invitations to speak at prestigious events such as annual conferences of major companies' senior managers, the annual conference of the UK Institute of Directors or the

World Economic Forum at Davos. You should be able to command a five-figure sum for each appearance.

The chat show

If your celebrity strategy has worked out well you will be invited as a guest on chat shows – minor ones at first, graduating finally to Parkinson or Oprah, than which there is no higher accolade in the celebrity world. The key to success here is two fold. On the one hand remember that your job is quite simply to make your audience laugh. So you must hire someone to write for you a whole batch of humorous anecdotes loosely based on your experience. The point is that they must be funny – they don't have to be true. The second key to success is that you must seize the initiative from the chat show's host. This is so you can tell the stories you want to rather than simply answer the host's questions. Here the tendency to domi- nate that you acquired during your business career may come in useful, but remember that your taking the initiative must appear to be the natural outcome of your charm and charisma.

You will probably need some coaching to achieve this effect.

A touch of class

You can afford to do one job for no financial reward, but one that will add even further to your overall reputation as one of the good as well as the great. Possibilities include chairing a major charity or a body such as Business for Social Responsibility.

Take your pick

The only remaining decisions are to do with your retirement lifestyle. The choice is almost unlimited. You could sail the Mediterranean in your own yacht, play on the world's most famous golf courses or soak up the sun in the Bahamas. As a world-class celebrity you can have Madonna or even the Prince of Wales as a house guest (though preferably not at the same time) and you can have your own table at the Ivy or the The Four Seasons. Whatever you choose you can relax knowing you can afford the best medical treatment in the world and that with luck you can look forward to twenty years of actively enjoying life. (Bear in mind the story of the man who won and then lost a fortune. When asked what went wrong he replied 'I spent half of it on wine, women and song'. 'What about the other half?' he was asked. 'Oh. I wasted it.' he replied.)

7. Epilogue

Obituary

The business community was shocked by the news of the sudden and untimely death of Sir Felix Catt, KBE. He apparently suffered a massive heart attack while on holiday in the Bahamas, but the exact circumstances of his death are not yet clear.

Family and friends are comforting his wife, who was not with him at the time.

Sir Felix was not only one of the most successful business leaders of our time, he was a strong supporter of the arts and of a number of worthy causes. As a person he was charmingly informal and well liked. He will be greatly missed.

His achievements in business are well known. Focusing on shareholder value he took the helm at successive companies that were delivering mediocre performance and, by stripping out costs, closing plants, moving production overseas and reducing manpower, saw their stock prices rise sharply. His final achievement in the business world was to negotiate the huge merger between his own company and Megalith Inc. It reflects well on the nature of the man that he declined the invitation to head up the combined company, choosing instead to retire at the height of his reputation. He was saddened to see the subsequent decline of the merged businesses and Megalith's application for Chapter 11 protection.

Since retiring from busines he had established a reputation as a raconteur and media personality, writing a succession of best selling books, appearing on chat shows on both sides of the Atlantic and presenting a series of TV productions with a business theme. He could count Royalty, top sports and show business personalities as well as heads of goverment among his many friends.

He was a man of many parts. He liked to revisit his roots in Ireland where he liked nothing better than to join the boys in the back room for an evening of Irish folk music, playing with a Gaelic band. Few people in the City knew what an accomplished fiddler he was.

A memorial service will be held at St Martins in the Fields on April 1st.